DRAWING
SERGE PELLÉ

SCRIPT
SYLVAIN RUNBERG

ORBITAL

3. NOMADS

CINEBOOK
The 9th Art Publisher

Original title: Orbital 3 – Nomades

Original edition: © Dupuis, 2009
by Runberg & Pellé
www.dupuis.com
All rights reserved

English translation: © 2011 Cinebook Ltd

Translator: Jerome Saincantin
Lettering and text layout: Imadjinn
Printed in Spain by Just Colour Graphic

This edition first published in Great Britain in 2011 by
Cinebook Ltd
56 Beech Avenue
Canterbury, Kent
CT4 7TA
www.cinebook.com

A CIP catalogue record for this book
is available from the British Library

ISBN 978-1-84918-080-1

9th CINEBOOK
The 9th Art Publisher

WHAT A MESS!

WE JUST PULLED UP THE NETS...

THEY'RE ALL DEAD...

DRIED UP, OR BURNED... I AIN'T SURE.

WE DIDN'T CATCH A SINGLE LIVE FISH!

WHAT'S GOING ON, WEN LEE?

OUR GOVERNMENT ALLOWED FISHING TO RESUME BARELY TWO YEARS AGO...

THEY SAID THAT WITH CONFEDERATE BIOTECHNOLOGY, MALAYSIAN WATERS WOULD BE THE MOST BOUNTIFUL ON EARTH?!

AND UNTIL NOW, THEY WERE RIGHT.

LOOK AT OUR CATCH ...

IT'S STILL AS PLENTIFUL AS EVER...

... AND ALIVE.

4

MAYBE HU CHI'S CREW HAPPENED UPON A PARASITE... SOME BUG FROM THE MANGROVE SWAMPS?

WE'VE GOT TO WARN HEALTH AUTHORITIES IN KUALA LUMPUR...

THEY OUGHT TO KNOW...?

WEN LEE!!

COME SEE!

THERE'S SOMETHING HUGE HEADING RIGHT FOR US!

IT'S GOING TO GET CAUGHT IN OUR NETS!

RELEASE THE WINCH!

SHUT OFF THE ANTI-G!!

SHUT OFF THE ANTI-G!!

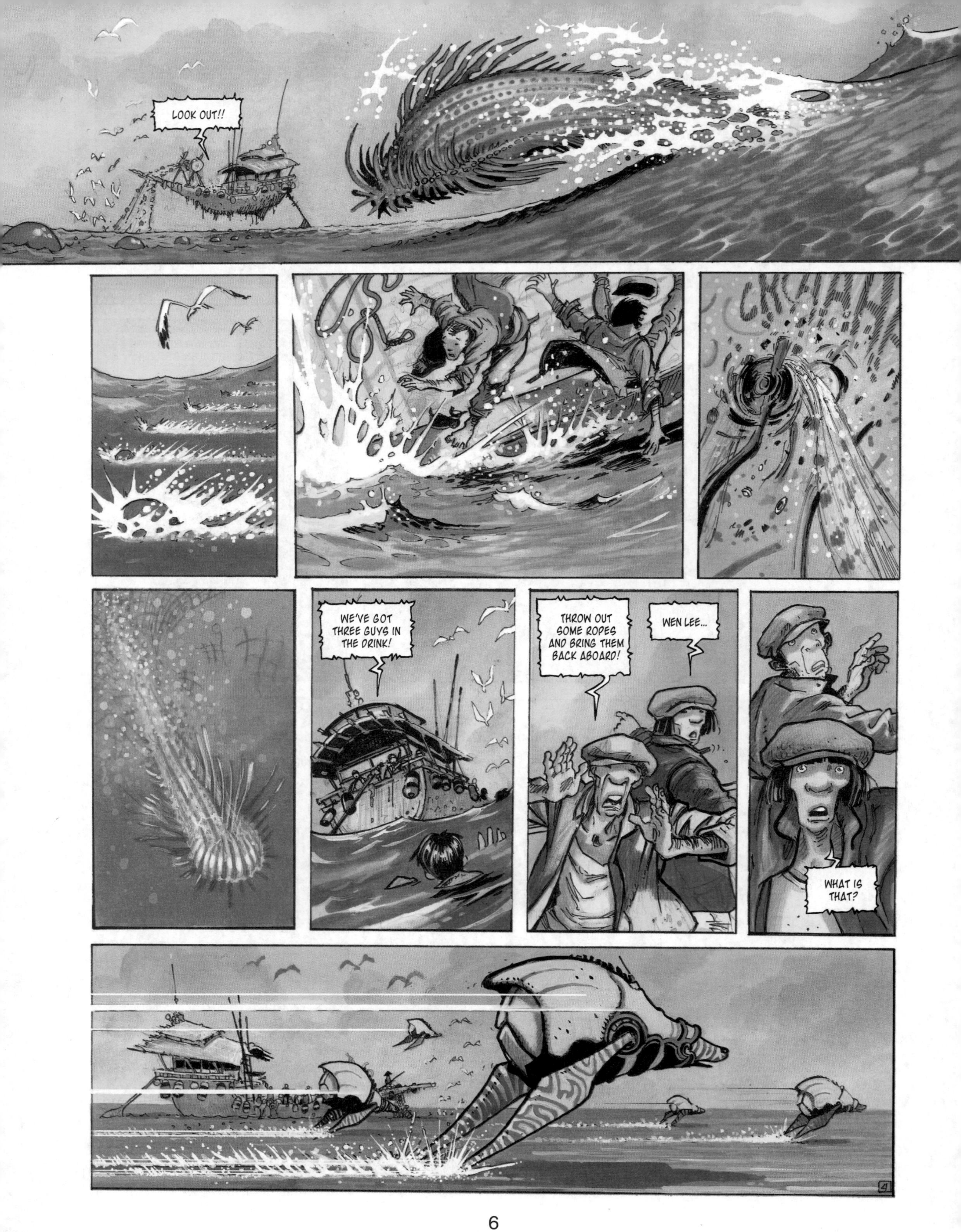

LOOK OUT!!
WE'VE GOT THREE GUYS IN THE DRINK!
THROW OUT SOME ROPES AND BRING THEM BACK ABOARD!
WEN LEE...
WHAT IS THAT?

I DUNNO, BUT WHAT'S FOR SURE...

...IS THAT IT'S NOT FROM AROUND HERE!

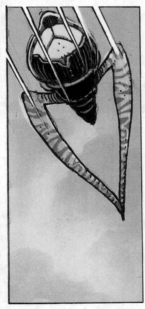

WARN HU CHI AND HIS GUYS...

WE HAVE TO GET OUT OF HERE!

CALEB SWANY.

I ALWAYS KNEW THAT THE IDO UNIFORM WOULD LOOK GREAT ON YOU!

MY DEAR HECTOR...

THE TRUTH IS, WITHOUT YOU...

I WOULDN'T BE WEARING IT!

AND I SUPPOSE THIS IS DIPLOMAT-AGENT MEZOKE IZZUA!

MEZOKE, IN SPITE OF MY 60 YEARS...

... ALLOW ME TO BOW BEFORE SUCH GRACE!

BEING YOUR ELDER BY SEVERAL DOZEN YEARS, MAYBE IT IS I WHO SHOULD BE BOWING, COLONEL ULRICH...

?

I IMAGINE I STILL HAVE QUITE A LOT TO LEARN ABOUT OUR SANDJARR FRIENDS...

YOU HAVE NO IDEA!

WHEN I HEARD THAT THE THREE OF US HAD BEEN PUT IN CHARGE OF SECURITY FOR THIS CEREMONY...

I KNOW, I KNOW...

FIFTEEN YEARS AFTER THAT STUPID, MURDEROUS WAR...

THE PRIME DIGNITARY DEEMED IT PROPER TO REUNITE US FOR THE OCCASION, AND I'M GRATEFUL FOR IT.

AT LAST, HUMAN/SANDJARR RECONCILIATION BECOMES A REALITY!

MY FRIENDS, WE WILL MAKE THE KUALA LUMPUR CEREMONIES AN UNFORGETTABLE SUCCESS!

AND THE MONUMENT THAT THIS KOROID ARTIST IS CREATING FOR THE OCCASION...

I NEVER GET TIRED OF SEEING HIM WORK!

THIS SCULPTURE WILL BE THE PRIDE OF BOTH OUR PEOPLES!

IS SOMETHING WRONG?

PARDON ME FOR INTERRUPTING...

THE MALAYSIAN COAST GUARD JUST SENT US AN ALERT!

ALIEN SHIPS HAVE BEEN LOCATED IN THE MANGROVE FORESTS, NEAR THE FISHING ZONES...

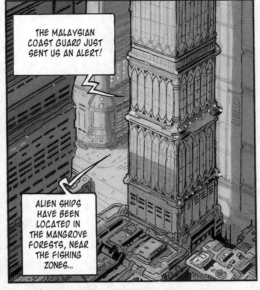

THERE'S ALREADY BEEN ONE INCIDENT INVOLVING LOCAL SAILORS!

WHICH ALIENS ARE WE TALKING ABOUT HERE?

APPARENTLY, SOME RAPAKHUN CLANS.

THE... RAPAKHUN? COULD YOU TELL ME MORE?

NOMADS; THEIR DISCRETION IS ON A PAR WITH THEIR BAD REPUTATION... THEY'RE WANDERERS.

THEY'VE ALWAYS REFUSED TO BE REPRESENTED AT THE CONFEDERATE ASSEMBLY.

ALSO, THE RAPAKHUN...

SCRATCH

YES?

THE RAPAKHUN ARE CANNIBALS...

THE FISHERMEN ALREADY HAVE AROUND 20 BOATS ON SITE...

THEY WANT TO ENTER THE ZONE WHERE THE RAPAKHUN HAVE SETTLED.

THE MALAYSIAN NAVY IS BLOCKING THEM WITH THREE CRUISERS, BUT, WELL...

THE RISK OF CONFLICT IS OBVIOUS.

AND TO MAKE THINGS EVEN BETTER...

THE REPRESENTATIVE OF THE FISHERMEN PRESSURED THE LOCAL GOVERNMENT INTO COMING WITH US WHEN WE MEET THE NOMADS.

I'M NOT SURE THIS IS GOING TO HELP US MUCH.

M'YEAH...

CREAK

CREAK

IN OTHER WORDS, IT ALL SMELLS VERY FISHY.

IS IT THAT IMPORTANT?

BESIDES, WHAT ARE THOSE FISHERMEN WORRIED ABOUT?

IF THE RAPAKHUN ARE CANNIBALS...

... THEY WON'T BE GOING AFTER HUMANS!

AN ECOLOGICAL DANGER OF ALIEN ORIGIN COULD HAVE CONSEQUENCES FOR THE RECONCILIATION CEREMONIES...

ESPECIALLY IN AN AREA WHERE FISHING HAS JUST RESUMED.

OBVIOUSLY, SOME OF THE LOCAL POPULATION IS COUNTING ON THIS VERY MUCH TO IMPROVE ITS DAILY LIFE.

AND THE RAPAKHUN HAVE A REPUTATION FOR VIOLENCE. IT'S NOTHING NEW.

AND IT'S UNFOUNDED.

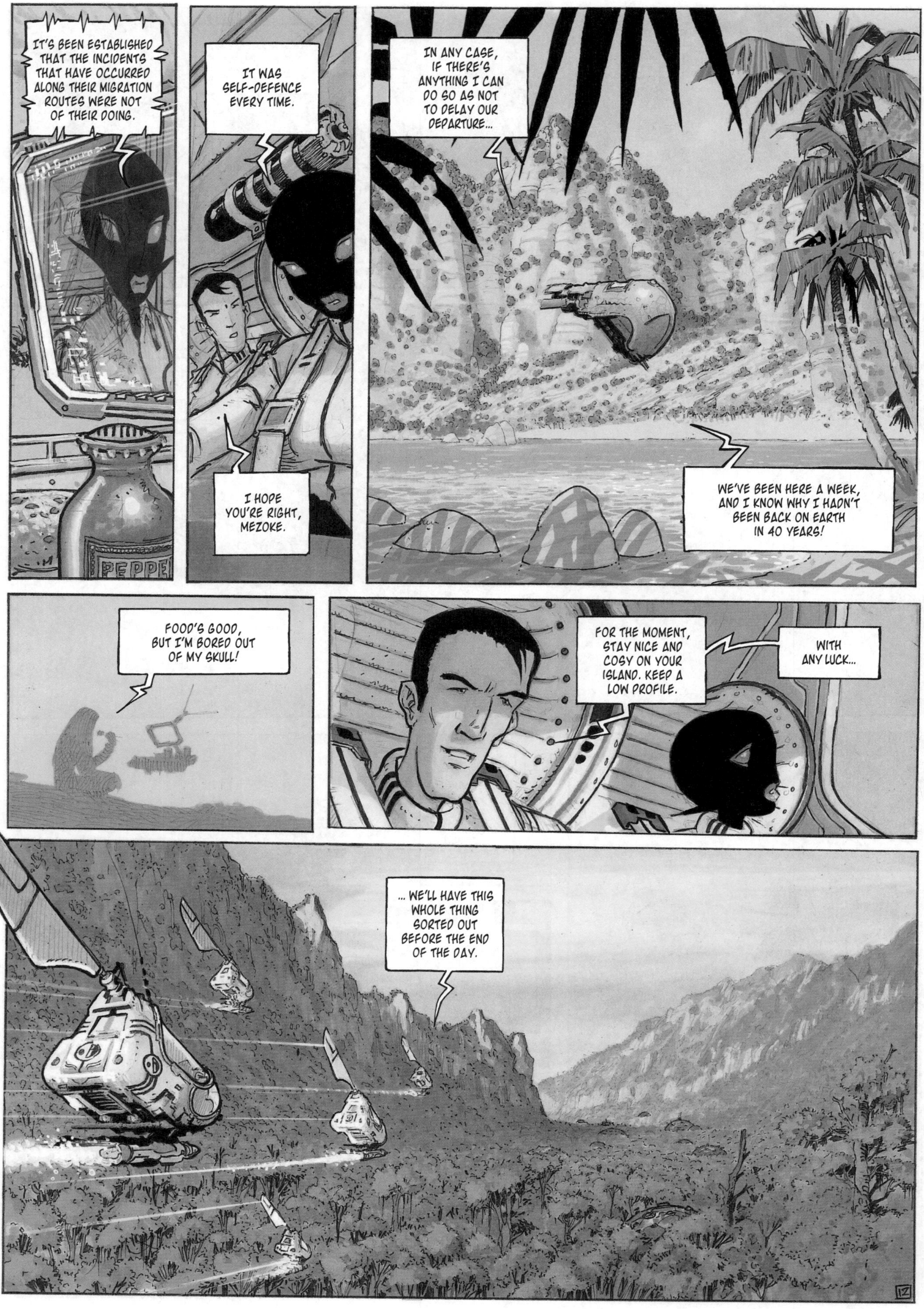
IT'S BEEN ESTABLISHED THAT THE INCIDENTS THAT HAVE OCCURRED ALONG THEIR MIGRATION ROUTES WERE NOT OF THEIR DOING.
IT WAS SELF-DEFENCE EVERY TIME.
I HOPE YOU'RE RIGHT, MEZOKE.
PEPPE
IN ANY CASE, IF THERE'S ANYTHING I CAN DO SO AS NOT TO DELAY OUR DEPARTURE...
WE'VE BEEN HERE A WEEK, AND I KNOW WHY I HADN'T BEEN BACK ON EARTH IN 40 YEARS!
FOOD'S GOOD, BUT I'M BORED OUT OF MY SKULL!
FOR THE MOMENT, STAY NICE AND COSY ON YOUR ISLAND. KEEP A LOW PROFILE.
WITH ANY LUCK...
... WE'LL HAVE THIS WHOLE THING SORTED OUT BEFORE THE END OF THE DAY.

MY NAME IS ALKUUN.

I ALONE, AMONG OUR CLAN, AM EQUIPPED WITH A TRANSLATOR IMPLANT...

THEREFORE, I SHALL SERVE AS OUR SPOKESWOMAN.

YOU UNDERSTAND US? WELL, YOU'D BETTER EXPLAIN YOURSELF, THEN!!!

!?

!?

THREE OF MY GUYS DARNED NEAR DROWNED, MY NETS ARE ALL BUSTED...

AND WE LOST SEVERAL TONS OF FISH!

AND THAT'S ALL YOUR FAULT!

13

ALKUUN... PLEASE FORGIVE THIS MAN'S VEHEMENCE.

HIS PEOPLE HAVE BEEN THROUGH DIFFICULT TIMES...

BUT IF WE CAME TO YOU, IT'S TO FIND A SOLUTION ...

... TOGETHER.

IF THE ELOKARN THAT ESCAPED FROM ITS PEN CAUSED YOU DIFFICULTIES, I AM SORRY ABOUT IT...

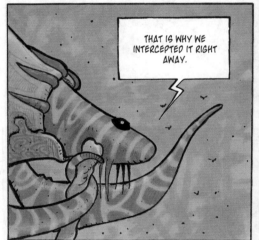

THAT IS WHY WE INTERCEPTED IT RIGHT AWAY.

EVER SINCE WE LEFT THE DEHADATO SYSTEM, THE HERD HAS BEEN PARTICULARLY AGITATED...

A CONUNDRUM. THEY ARE USUALLY OF A PLACID DISPOSITION.

THE CHANGE OF PLANET MAY HAVE UPSET SOME OF THEM. IT HAPPENS SOMETIMES...

BUT ONE THING IS CERTAIN... WE HAVE NOTHING TO DO WITH...

... WHAT HAS AFFECTED YOUR FISHING PRESERVES!

OUR TEAMS ARE CURRENTLY TAKING SAMPLES ON SITE...

WE SHOULD SOON BE ABLE TO DETERMINE WHAT CAUSED THOSE ANIMALS' DEATHS.

BUT CONSIDERING YOUR PRESENCE AT THE LOCATION, IT WAS NATURAL THAT WE CONTACT YOU TO DISCUSS THE SITUATION.

WE RESPECT THE WORLDS WE VISIT.

ALL OF THEM...

... WITHOUT EXCEPTION.

THE GODS OF THE STARS ARE NUMBERLESS, AS ARE THE RICHES THEY OFFER US.

FOLLOW ME, AND YOU WILL SEE THAT WE HONOUR YOURS ALSO!

WE TAKE, BUT WE ALSO GIVE BACK... EVERY TIME WE SETTLE ONTO A NEW WORLD.

ONE OF US IS GOING TO OFFER HIS LIFE FORCE TO YOUR PLANET.

HIS SOUL WILL NOURISH YOUR GODS...

... AND HIS BODY THE ELDERS OF OUR CLAN.

BUT... HE... HE'S ALIVE?

OF COURSE.

IT IS WITH LIFE THAT WE CELEBRATE LIFE. AND IT IS AN HONOUR I WILL KNOW AS WELL...

I WILL BE THE ONE WHO OFFERS MYSELF TO THE STAR SPIRITS WHEN NEXT WE TRAVEL.

DEWEI? YOU OK?

IT'S... THAT SMELL... I WANT TO LEAVE...

IS SOMETHING WRONG?

LIKE YOU, HUMANS ARE SENSITIVE TO SPIRITUAL THINGS. SOMETIMES EVEN...

... TOO MUCH SO...

IT CAN IMPACT THEIR PHYSICAL ABILITIES.

WE THANK YOU FOR SEEING US.

AS SOON AS WE HAVE RECEIVED THE TEST RESULTS...

... WE WILL FORWARD THEM TO YOU. AFTER ALL...

... WHAT KILLED THE FISH MIGHT PROVE DANGEROUS TO YOU AS WELL.

WHILE CALEB AND MEZOKE SPOKE WITH THE NOMADS, I CONTACTED THE MALAYSIAN NAVAL FORCES.

UNTIL THE CLOSING OF THE CEREMONIES, THEY'LL LEAVE SEVERAL SHIPS POSTED NEAR THE MANGROVE FOREST WHERE WE'RE CONDUCTING THE SEARCH, SO AS TO AVOID ANY INCIDENTS WITH THE RAPAKHUN.

AND I'LL CONTINUE TO SUPERVISE THE OPERATIONS ON SITE...

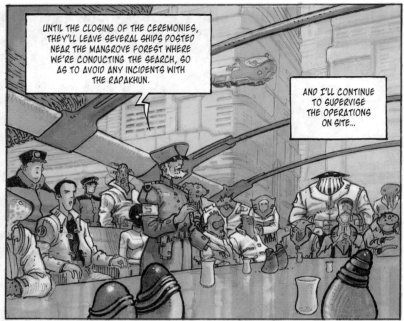

AS FOR US, WEN LEE AGREED TO DRAW HIS BOATS BACK AND SUSPEND FISHING OPERATIONS FOR 48 HOURS IN ORDER TO MAKE THINGS EASIER FOR US. BUT HE REALLY DIDN'T LIKE IT!

THE AUTHORITIES OF KUALA LUMPUR HAVE STATIONED SEVERAL POLICE UNITS NEAR THE HARBOUR, IN CASE OF CLASHES WITH THE FISHERMEN...

I HOPE IT WON'T COME TO THAT!

DO YOU THINK IT COULD STILL SPIRAL OUT OF CONTROL? THE RAPAKHUN DENIED ANY INVOLVEMENT!

UNTIL WE HAVE THE TEST RESULTS, WE ONLY HAVE THEIR WORD AS PROOF OF THEIR GOOD FAITH.

CONSIDERING THE CIRCUMSTANCES, I DOUBT THAT'LL BE ENOUGH TO APPEASE THE FISHERMEN...

ESPECIALLY AFTER THE SACRIFICE THAT WEN LEE WITNESSED BACK THERE!

YOUR REMARK IS UNFAIR...

EVEN IF THOSE HUMANS CAN'T STAND WHAT THEY DON'T UNDERSTAND, IT DOESN'T GIVE THEM ANY RIGHT TO JUDGE THE RAPAKHUN!

I KNOW, MEZOKE...

I'M JUST SAYING THAT IT WAS A MISTAKE TO BRING THEM WITH US.

ALL WE DID WAS ACCEDE TO THEIR DEMAND!

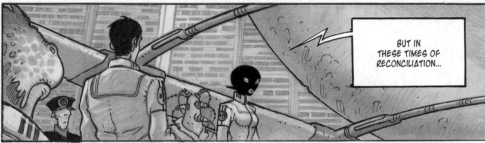

BUT IN THESE TIMES OF RECONCILIATION...

IT SEEMS THAT TRUSTING NON-HUMANS IS STILL SOMEWHAT UTOPIAN ON YOUR PLANET!

19

21

OUR HEAVY TRANSPORTS ARE AT THE IDO'S DISPOSAL FOR THE DURATION OF THE CEREMONY.

YOU'LL BE ABLE TO PARK YOUR OWN AIRCRAFT THERE.

AND YOU'LL HAVE THE SUPPORT OF OUR MAINTENANCE TEAMS IF NEED BE.

LIEUTENANT, THE HELP THAT THE MALAYSIAN MILITARY IS OFFERING US IS MORE THAN USEFUL...

WE THANK YOU SINCERELY FOR YOUR COOPERATION!

IT'S AN HONOUR TO SERVE THE CONFEDERATE CAUSE THUS!

IF YOU'LL EXCUSE ME, I STILL HAVE SOME DETAILS TO ATTEND TO...

MEZOKE?

EVERYTHING ALL RIGHT ON YOUR SIDE?

I CHECKED THE ANTI-G VIDEO SYSTEM...

THERE ARE CLOSE TO 300 DROIDS PATROLLING THE AREA FULL-TIME...

YOU CAN REST EASY, CALEB SWANY. YOUR PARTY IS UNDER CONTROL.

LISTEN...

I THOUGHT YOU WOULD APPRECIATE THIS EVENT THE WAY I DO...

AND I GET THE FEELING THAT'S NOT THE CASE.

YOU'RE CORRECT.

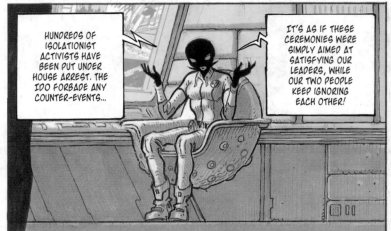

HUNDREDS OF ISOLATIONIST ACTIVISTS HAVE BEEN PUT UNDER HOUSE ARREST. THE IDO FORBADE ANY COUNTER-EVENTS...

IT'S AS IF THESE CEREMONIES WERE SIMPLY AIMED AT SATISFYING OUR LEADERS, WHILE OUR TWO PEOPLE KEEP IGNORING EACH OTHER!

BUT THE SANDJARR DELEGATION WILL ARRIVE ON EARTH TOMORROW. THEY REPRESENT YOUR PEOPLE!

ALLOW ME TO DOUBT THAT...

CALEB SWANY?

YES?

HEY, BUDDY!

LUKAS VESELY?

WHAT ARE YOU DOING HERE? I DON'T BELIEVE IT!

I'M PART OF THE SECURITY FORCE LED BY OLD ULRICH...

SEE? I'VE GOT A CAREER, TOO...

EVEN IF I HAVEN'T QUITE REACHED THE SAME HEIGHTS YOU HAVE.

MEZOKE, MAY I INTRODUCE LUKAS...

WE MET IN PRAGUE WHEN I WAS A TEENAGER...

IT... IT'S WEIRD TO SEE YOU HERE...

NO STRANGER THAN HEARING ABOUT YOU JOINING THE IDO.

AFTER WHAT WE WENT THROUGH TOGETHER, I WAS... SURPRISED.

REALLY, VERY SURPRISED.

NOTHING THAT MATTERS ANYMORE. RIGHT, CALEB?

AND WHAT WAS IT YOU WENT THROUGH TOGETHER?

HERE, THIS IS MY NUMBER.

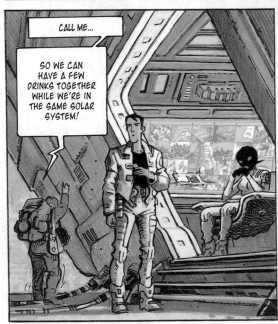

CALL ME...

SO WE CAN HAVE A FEW DRINKS TOGETHER WHILE WE'RE IN THE SAME SOLAR SYSTEM!

YOU DIDN'T ANSWER MY QUESTION...

LUKAS DID.

IT DOESN'T MATTER.

DOESN'T MATTER AT ALL.

KEEP RUNNING!

THIS WAY!

MILO-O-OS ?!!

WELL, WHAT'S WRONG WITH YOU 1608 YOUTH, THEN?

DON'T WANT TO PLAY WITH US ANYMORE?

MILOS?! ANSWER ME!

YEAAAH! YOU CAUGHT THEM!

WELL... WHAT ARE WE GOING TO DO WITH YOU?

BECAUSE, REALLY...

FREE HUMANITY FROM ALIEN AUTHORIT

JOIN HE ISOLATION

00 87 0142 37520

IT WASN'T TOO SMART, PUTTING UP YOUR STINKING POSTERS AROUND HERE!

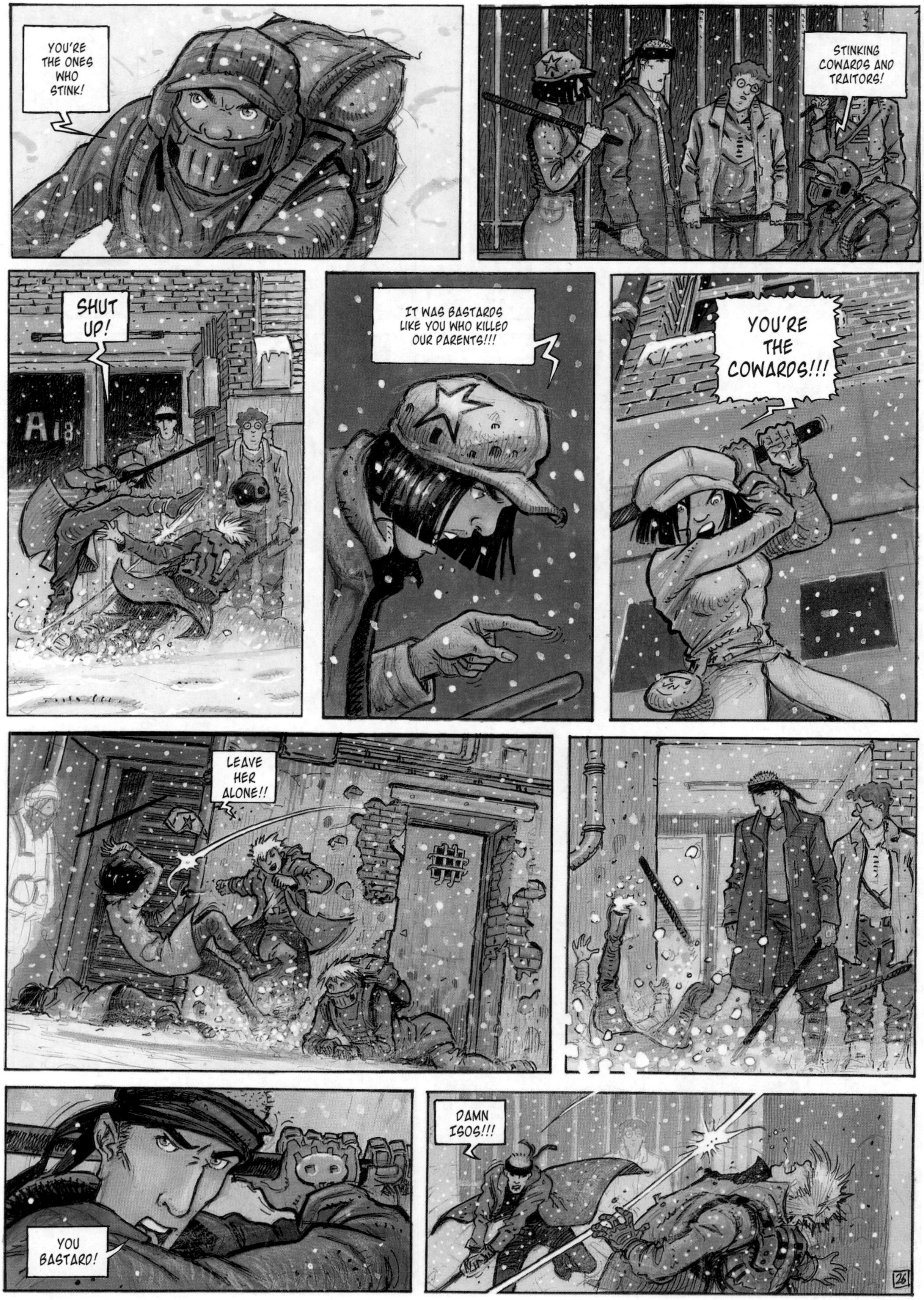
YOU'RE THE ONES WHO STINK!
STINKING COWARDS AND TRAITORS!
SHUT UP!
IT WAS BASTARDS LIKE YOU WHO KILLED OUR PARENTS!!!
YOU'RE THE COWARDS!!!
LEAVE HER ALONE!!
YOU BASTARD!
DAMN ISOS!!!
26

KRISTINA! CALEB! THE COPS ARE HERE!

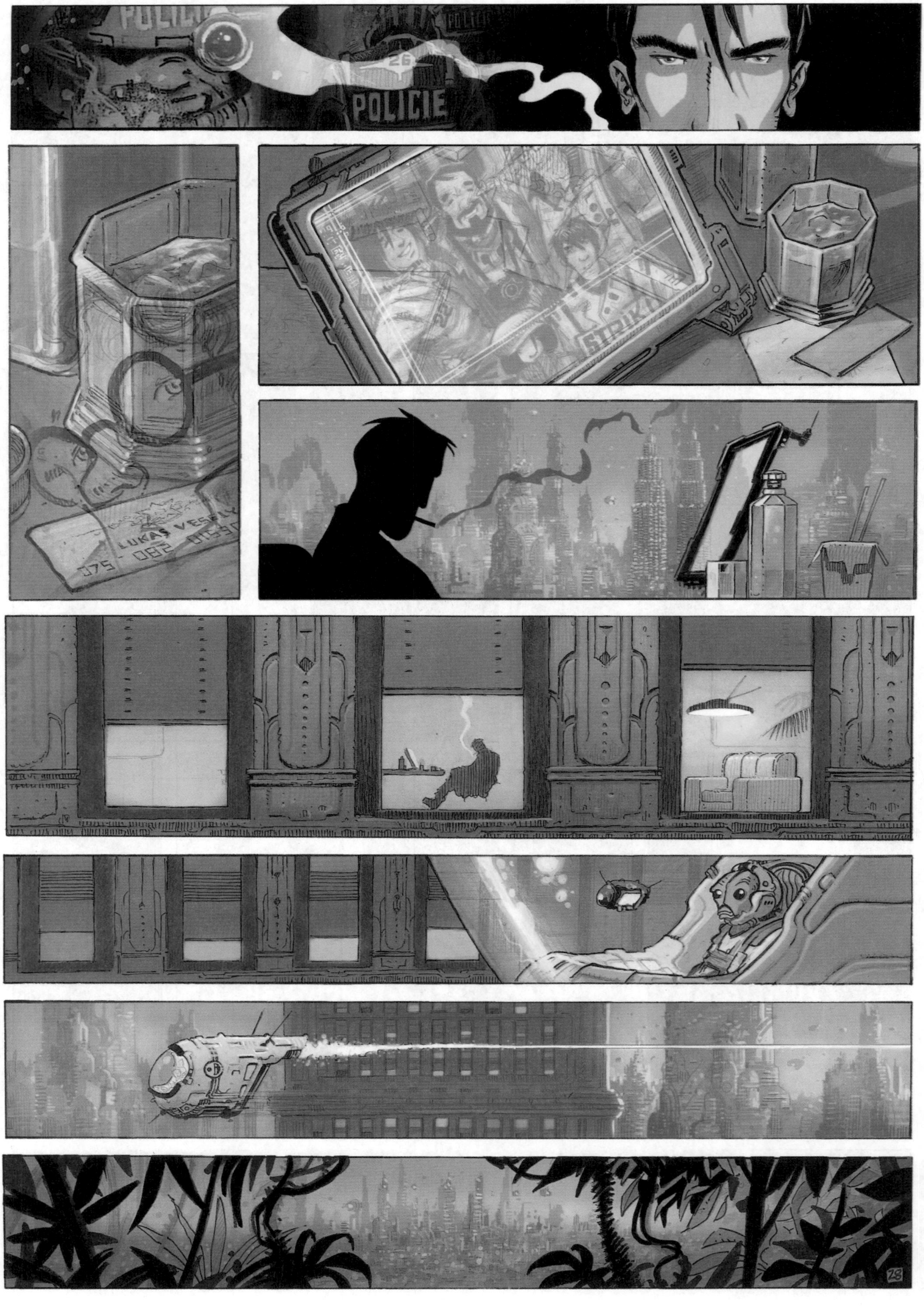
POLICIE

MAN! WHAT WAS THE POINT OF TAKING ALL THOSE RISKS?

SNEAKING INSIDE THE FORBIDDEN ZONE... FOR WHAT?

A WHOLE BUNCH OF DEAD FISH!

WEN LEE DID WARN US...

YEAH, BUT WE'D HAVE REGRETTED IT IF WE HADN'T TRIED, RIGHT?

SURE... WHAT WE REALLY NEED IS TO GET OUT OF HERE BEFORE WE'RE SPOTTED...

I'M RESTARTING THE ENGINES!

LOOK WHO'S WATCHING US OVER THERE...

THE ALIENS THAT KILLED OUR FISH!

WE'VE GOT TO GRAB THEM AND BRING THEM BACK TO PORT!

WHAT FOR? THAT'S JUST STUPID!

NO, IT'S A GREAT OPPORTUNITY.

WE'RE GOING TO BRING PROOF THAT THOSE FREAKS ARE RESPONSIBLE FOR ALL OF THIS!

WE ALMOST HAVE THEM!!

STAND READY ON THE NETS!

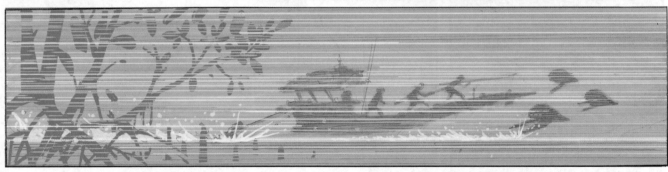

THIS IS THE RADAR CONTACT THAT THE MALAYSIAN NAVY DETECTED.

AT FIRST, THEY THOUGHT IT WAS ONE OF OUR VEHICLES...

YOU MUST BE KIDDING?!

I DON'T KNOW WHAT THOSE MORONS ARE DOING HERE...

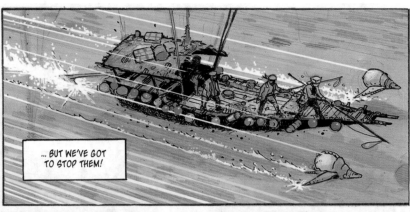

... BUT WE'VE GOT TO STOP THEM!

CUT THEM OFF...

IF ANYTHING HAPPENS TO THOSE RAPAKHUN, IT'LL BE A DISASTER!

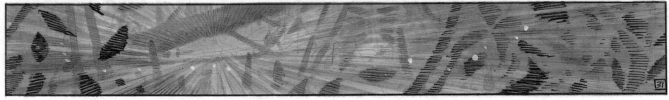

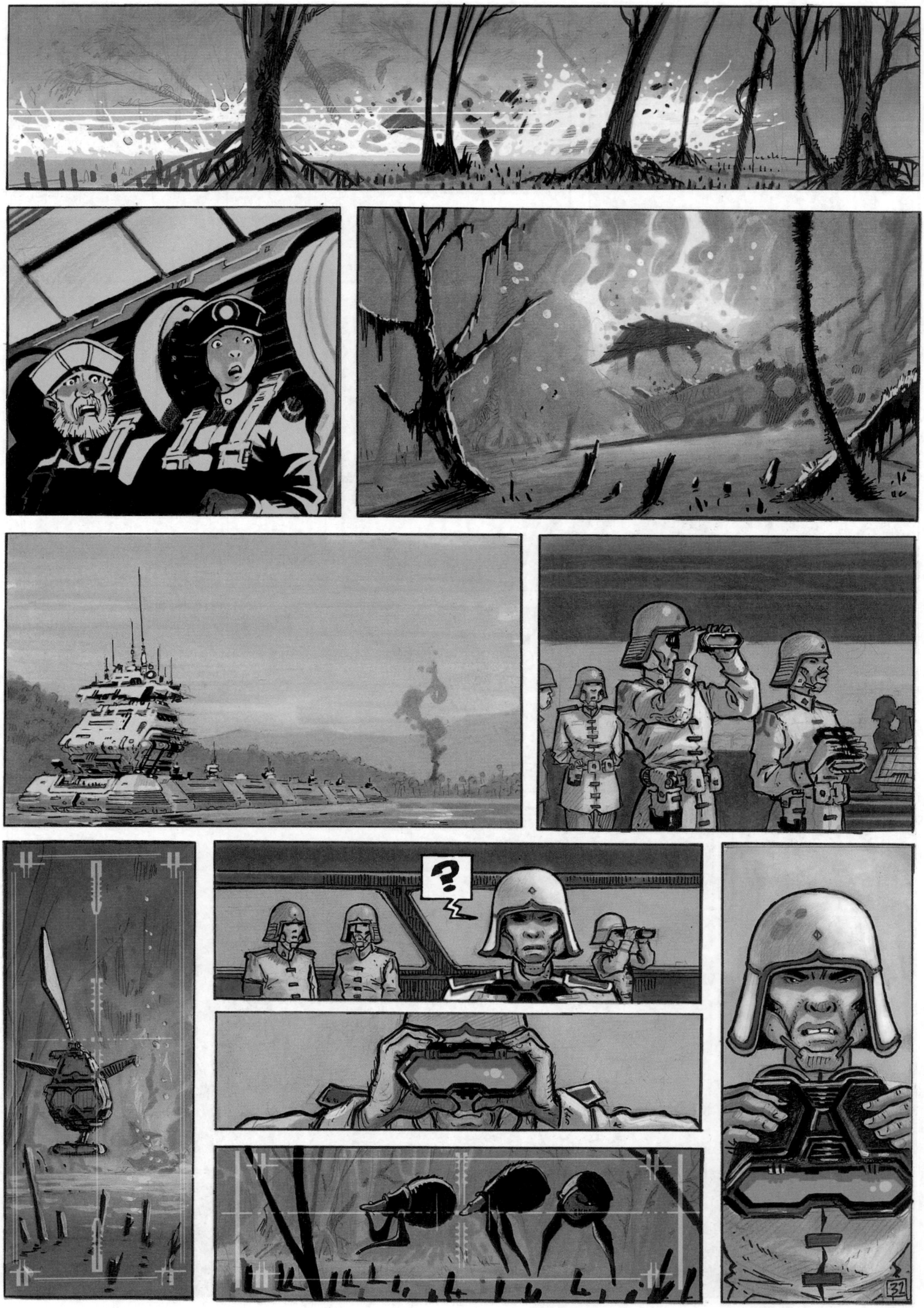
?
32

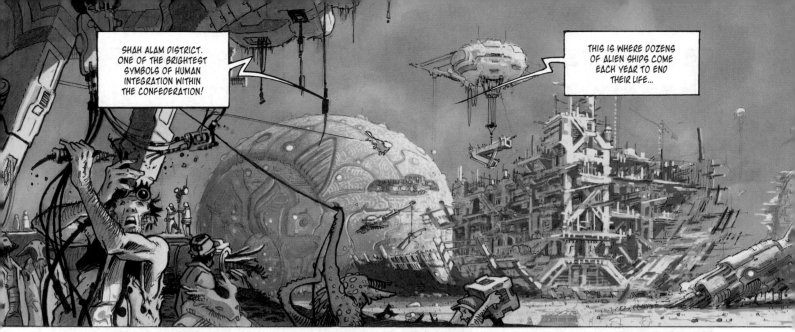

SHAH ALAM DISTRICT. ONE OF THE BRIGHTEST SYMBOLS OF HUMAN INTEGRATION WITHIN THE CONFEDERATION!

THIS IS WHERE DOZENS OF ALIEN SHIPS COME EACH YEAR TO END THEIR LIFE...

HERE, THEY ARE TAKEN APART BY THE EXPERT HANDS OF THE LOCAL SCRAPPERS.

AND, OVER THE YEARS, THIS AREA OF KUALA LUMPUR HAS BECOME A TRUE MIXED DISTRICT, HUMANS AND ALIENS...

A PLACE OF PEACEFUL COHABITATION, ANCHORED IN INTERPLANETARY ECONOMIC DEVELOPMENT.

AND THIS COOPERATION ALSO TOOK ON OTHER ASPECTS, MORE ECOLOGICAL IN NATURE.

35

JUST 15 YEARS AGO, THE MALAYSIAN SEA FLOOR WAS DYING OFF BECAUSE OF SEVERAL CENTURIES OF ACCUMULATED POLLUTION...

FISHING HAD BECOME A MARGINAL ACTIVITY AND SEA LIFE WAS DISAPPEARING LITTLE BY LITTLE.

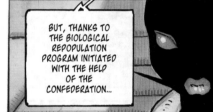

BUT, THANKS TO THE BIOLOGICAL REPOPULATION PROGRAM INITIATED WITH THE HELP OF THE CONFEDERATION...

... ALIEN CLONING TECHNOLOGIES SUCCEEDED IN BRINGING BACK TO LIFE ALMOST THE WHOLE UNDERWATER ECOSYSTEM, WHICH UNTIL THEN WAS SLATED FOR THE WORST.

EXTINCT SPECIES WERE REINTRODUCED...

... AND FISHING DEVELOPED ONCE AGAIN, OFFERING THE LOCAL POPULATION YET MORE ECONOMIC OPPORTUNITIES.

SOME BOATS WERE EVEN EQUIPPED RECENTLY WITH ANTI-G TECHNOLOGY SO THEY COULD GO NEAR THE SHALLOWS SAFELY.

I THINK IT'S IMPORTANT TO MENTION THAT ISOLATIONIST INFLUENCE WAS ALWAYS VERY LOW IN THIS COUNTRY.

SO YOU'LL UNDERSTAND WHY THESE MANY ACCOMPLISHMENTS OF KUALA LUMPUR MADE IT THE IDEAL CITY IN WHICH TO CELEBRATE THE RECONCILIATION OF OUR TWO PEOPLE.

OUR THANKS, DIPLOMAT.

THIS RECEPTION SHOWED US YOUR PLANET IN AN UNEXPECTED LIGHT!

MEZOKE, ONE LAST WORD BEFORE WE HEAD FOR THE OFFICIAL RESIDENCE WHERE YOUR PEOPLE CAN GET SETTLED?

NO.

I HAVE NOTHING TO ADD.

LET THEM GO AND REST.

FOUR FISHERMEN DEAD?

SCHLOOK

BAD NEWS.

PLOF

FOR THE CEREMONY.

NO?

HECTOR, THE WATER AND FISH SAMPLES GAVE US NOTHING...

NO POISON.

NO VIRUS...

NO BACTERIA...

THE FISH WERE EXPOSED TO AN AS-YET-UNIDENTIFIED ENERGY SOURCE, WHICH DESTROYED THEIR LIFE ENERGY.

AND THERE'S SOMETHING ELSE, TOO.

IT'S ABOUT THE MOON SENESTAM...

THE JÄVLODS HAVE ABANDONED THEIR MINING OPERATION...

BECAUSE OF THE STILVULLS THAT HAD BEEN TEEMING THERE FOR MONTHS. SO, WE EVACUATED THE HUMAN COLONY FOR NOTHING.

AS FOR THE NEW LEADER OF THEIR GOVERNMENT, SENZER WOOL, HE WAS FOUND DEAD THIS MORNING.

SUICIDE.

OR SO I HEARD.

THERE ARE RUMOURS THAT HIS FORMER ACHEROD ALLIES MADE HIM PAY FOR HIS LATE CHANGE OF MIND...

THOSE RUMOURS ARE IMPOSSIBLE TO VERIFY. WE'LL LET THEM DIE OUT ON THEIR OWN!

LET'S GET BACK TO THOSE FISHERMEN.

WHAT DO YOU PROPOSE, COLONEL ULRICH?

WE HAVE TO PRESENT IT AS A SIMPLE ACCIDENT.

THEY LOST CONTROL OF THEIR JUNK AND CRASHED INTO THE MANGROVE FOREST.

AS FOR THE PRESENCE OF COLONEL ULRICH AND THE RAPAKHUN, WHY MENTION IT?

IT WAS AN ACCIDENT, WASN'T IT?

INVOLVING FISHERMEN WHO WERE SAILING IN AN AREA WHERE THEY SHOULD NOT HAVE BEEN...

THAT... THAT'S TRUE.

TONIGHT, EARTH'S GOVERNMENT IS GOING TO MEET THE SANDJARR DIGNITARIES BEFORE THE CEREMONY.

NOTHING MUST CAST A SHADOW ON THIS MEETING.

SO, LET'S DO WHAT WE HAVE TO DO TO MAKE SURE THE HARBOUR PEOPLE STAY PUT!

WE'RE SORRY ABOUT WHAT HAPPENED.

THE IDO WOULD LIKE TO OFFER TO PAY ALL EXPENSES FOR THEIR FUNERALS, AS A SIGN OF SOLIDARITY.

WOULD YOU DO US THE HONOUR OF ACCEPTING?

NO.

WE CAN TAKE CARE OF OUR OWN.

I UNDERSTAND.

WE'LL LEAVE YOU NOW.

BOSS, THERE'S A NAVY MAN HERE TO SEE YOU...

... ABOUT WHAT HAPPENED IN THE MANGROVE FOREST.

I'M HERE AS A PATRIOT.

BECAUSE MY SUPERIORS AND THE IDO LIED TO YOU.

YOUR MEN WERE KILLED BY RAPAKHUN. I SAW IT ALL.

AND IF YOU WANT TO AVENGE THEIR DEATHS...

THERE ARE SEVERAL OF US IN THE NAVY WHO'D LIKE TO HELP YOU DO SO.

41

I DON'T UNDERSTAND.

WHY LIE ABOUT THE FISHERMEN?

TO PROTECT YOUR FRIEND?

HECTOR ISN'T GUILTY OF ANYTHING, ASIDE FROM BEING UNLUCKY.

IF I SUGGESTED WE ACT THIS WAY...

IF EVONA TOOT ACCEPTED MY OFFER...

IT'S FOR THEM!

EARTH'S FIVE CONTINENTAL LEADERS TALKING TO THE SANDJARR ELITE!

THE WHOLE THING BROADCAST LIVE BY ALL MAJOR CONFEDERATE MEDIA!

YOU STILL HAVE NOTHING TO SAY?

THAT ALL OF THIS IS POSSIBLE, AFTER THAT HORRIBLE WAR...

IT SHOULD MAKE YOU HAPPY!

WHAT'S YOUR PROBLEM, THEN?

YOU DIDN'T LISTEN TO ME.

MY PROBLEM IS THAT THESE PEOPLE...

... AREN'T MY PEOPLE.

43

THREE HYDROSHIPS WE REBUILT USING OLD GARMOZIAN SHIPS.

MUCH FASTER...

MUCH NIMBLER THAN YOUR ANTI-G JUNKS.

MY GUYS AND ME WERE PLANNING ON USING THEM TO EXPLORE THE OCEAN BOTTOM...

JUST TO SEE IF THERE MIGHT STILL BE SOME HUMAN SHIPWRECKS LYING ABOUT...

BUT, HEY.

CONSIDERING WHAT YOU TOLD US...

YOU HAVE MORE USE FOR THEM.

44

THANKS, RADVINUS.

I KNEW I COULD COUNT ON THE BEST ALIEN SCRAPPER IN SHAH ALAM!

PLEASE...

WE LIVE IN THE SAME CITY...

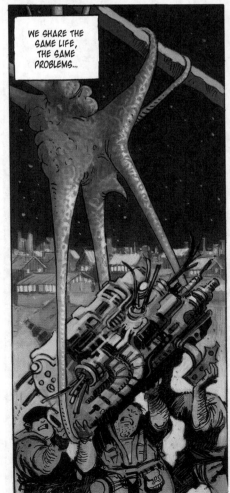

WE SHARE THE SAME LIFE, THE SAME PROBLEMS...

SO, HEY!

WE'VE GOT TO STICK TOGETHER...

WHEN SOME RAGTAG NOMADS COME AND MESS UP OUR HOME!

43

THE PREMIER CIRCLES?

OF COURSE I KNOW WHAT IT IS!

IT'S YOUR HIGHER ARISTOCRACY, THE LEADERS WHO RULE OVER YOUR PEOPLE.

THIRTEEN MEMBERS CHOSEN FOR 30-YEAR MANDATES...

NON-RENEWABLE MANDATES.

AN ARISTOCRACY TO WHICH THESE FIVE REPRESENTATIVES BELONG, ACTUALLY.

AN ARISTOCRACY I BELONGED TO AS WELL, BEFORE THE WAR.

WHAT?

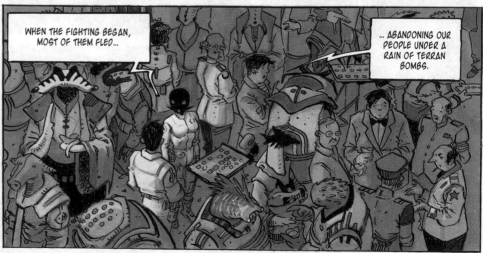

WHEN THE FIGHTING BEGAN, MOST OF THEM FLED...

... ABANDONING OUR PEOPLE UNDER A RAIN OF TERRAN BOMBS.

I REFUSED TO FOLLOW THEM.

44

I REMAINED BESIDE THOSE WE REPRESENTED.

THE SANDJARR PEOPLE.

AS ALL THE MEMBERS OF THE PREMIER CIRCLES SHOULD HAVE DONE.

I JOINED A MEDICAL TEAM; WE TRIED TO DEAL WITH THE MOST URGENT PROBLEMS...

OFTEN, THAT MEANT LITTLE MORE THAN BURYING THE BODIES AFTER HUMAN ATTACKS...

... TO PREVENT EPIDEMICS.

AFTER THE CONFLICT ENDED...

... THE MEMBERS OF THE PREMIER CIRCLES CAME BACK. THEY RESUMED RULING AS IF NOTHING HAD HAPPENED.

I RENOUNCED MY TITLES, WHICH MADE ME A GOOD MANY ENEMIES AMONG MY SPECIES.

AND EVENTUALLY...

... I DECIDED TO JOIN THE IDO.

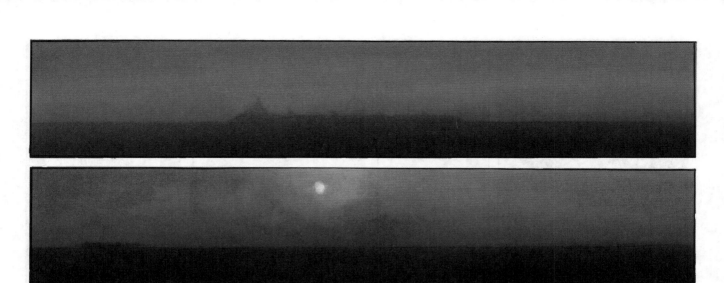

ARE YOU SURE THEY'LL DO AS THEY SAID THEY WOULD?

WE'RE ABOUT TO FIND OUT.

THEY SHOULD BE THROUGH BY NOW.

AND THEY SHOULDN'T HAVE BEEN SPOTTED.

GOOD. WE CAN RECONNECT THE RADAR, THEN.

WE'VE DONE IT.

JUSTICE IS GONNA BE SERVED!

I DIDN'T KNOW ANY OF THIS.

YOU HAD NO REASON TO.

I COULD HAVE BEEN A MEMBER OF THIS DELEGATION, HAD THINGS TAKEN A DIFFERENT PATH.

BUT INSTEAD...

... I'VE BECOME A LIVING SYMBOL OF THEIR GUILTY CONSCIENCE.

CALEB! MEZOKE!

OUR SATELLITES HAVE SPOTTED UNIDENTIFIED HYDROSHIPS OFF THE MANGROVE SWAMPS...

I CALLED THE MALAYSIAN NAVY; THEY DIDN'T SEE ANYTHING...

NO EXPLANATION!

THE RAPAKHUN...

WE HAVE TO PROTECT THE RAPAKHUN!

NOT MUCH FURTHER TO THEIR SHIPS, NOW.

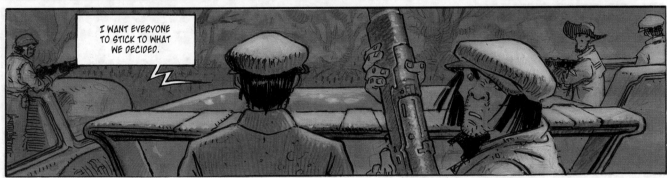

I WANT EVERYONE TO STICK TO WHAT WE DECIDED.

... WE WILL TAKE FOUR OF THEM.

FOR THE FOUR OF US THAT THEY KILLED...

NO MORE.

NO LESS.

IT LOOKS LIKE THERE'S SOMETHING AHEAD OF US...?

I CAN'T REALLY SEE...

AND THERE'S NOTHING ON THE NAVIGATION SCAN!

BUT IT DOESN'T LOOK LIKE...

HEY?!

IT'S COMING FROM THE SIDES, TOO!!!

AND ABOV...

IT'S EVERYWHERE!

THIS THING'S EVERYWHERE!!!

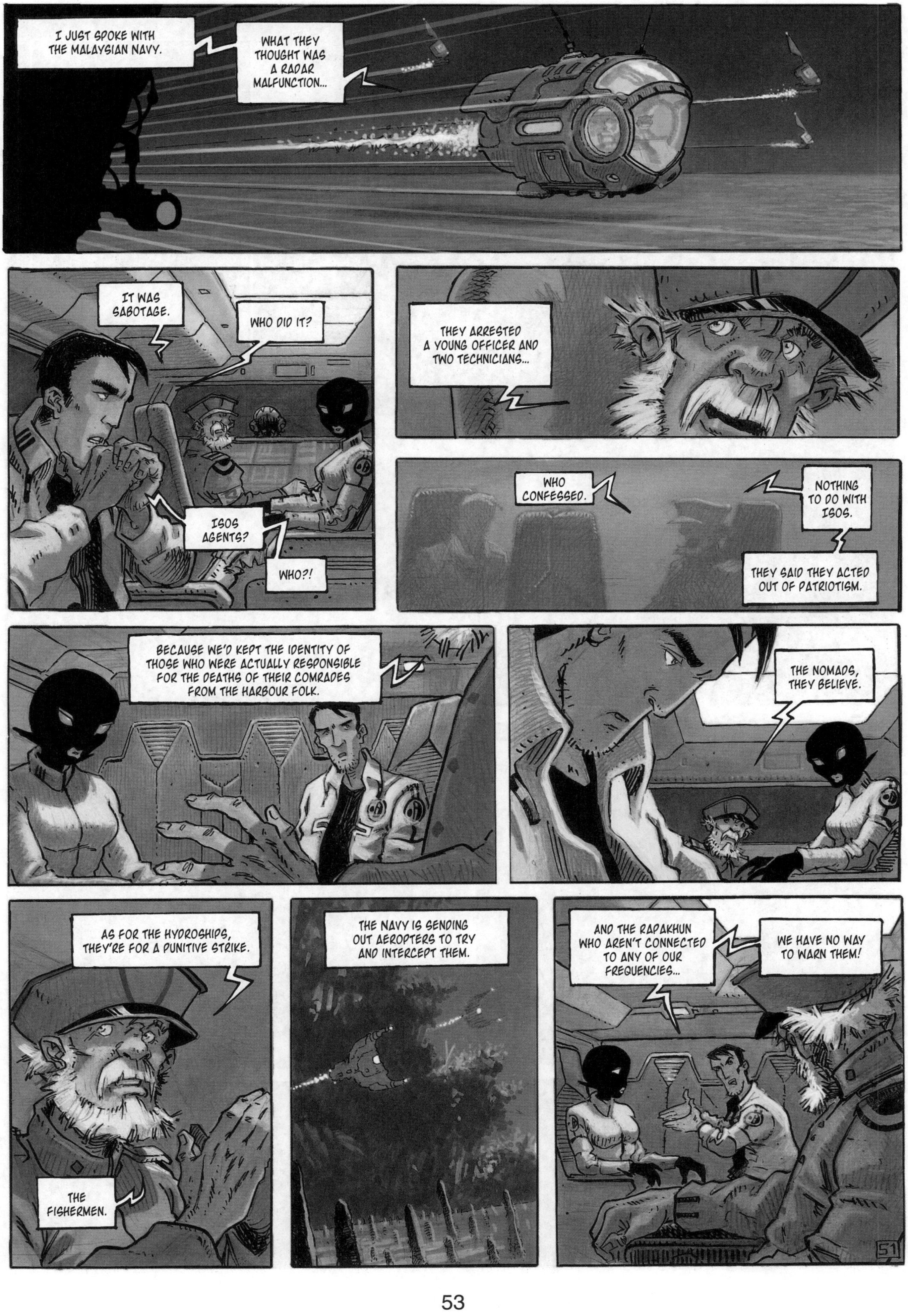

I JUST SPOKE WITH THE MALAYSIAN NAVY.
WHAT THEY THOUGHT WAS A RADAR MALFUNCTION...
IT WAS SABOTAGE.
WHO DID IT?
ISOS AGENTS?
WHO?!
THEY ARRESTED A YOUNG OFFICER AND TWO TECHNICIANS...
WHO CONFESSED.
NOTHING TO DO WITH ISOS.
THEY SAID THEY ACTED OUT OF PATRIOTISM.
BECAUSE WE'D KEPT THE IDENTITY OF THOSE WHO WERE ACTUALLY RESPONSIBLE FOR THE DEATHS OF THEIR COMRADES FROM THE HARBOUR FOLK.
THE NOMADS, THEY BELIEVE.
AS FOR THE HYDROSHIPS, THEY'RE FOR A PUNITIVE STRIKE.
THE FISHERMEN.
THE NAVY IS SENDING OUT AEROPTERS TO TRY AND INTERCEPT THEM.
AND THE RAPAKHUN WHO AREN'T CONNECTED TO ANY OF OUR FREQUENCIES...
WE HAVE NO WAY TO WARN THEM!
51

THE IDIOCY... IT'S GOING TO BE A SLAUGHTER!

WHAT HAPPENED HERE?

THE MILITARY HAS NO IDEA.

THE FISHERMEN WERE ALREADY DEAD WHEN THEY GOT HERE...

WHAT ABOUT THE RAPAKHUN...

... DO THEY HAVE ANYTHING TO TELL US?

SO?

THEY CLAIM TO KNOW NOTHING.

THEY ONLY DISCOVERED THE CARNAGE AFTER THE NAVY'S AEROPTERS ARRIVED.

ON THE OTHER HAND, I GOT A CALL FROM EVONA TOOT.

THE MEDIA PRESENT FOR THE PRE-CEREMONY RECEPTION HEARD ABOUT TROUBLE IN THE MANGROVE FORESTS.

WE'RE GOING TO HAVE TO GIVE THEM SOMETHING TO SATISFY THEIR CURIOSITY.

OK.

WE'VE GOT TO ACT FAST.

OTHERWISE...

...WE'RE HEAD-ED STRAIGHT FOR DISASTER.

53

55

I'LL TAKE CARE OF KEEPING THE MEDIANAUTS AT BAY.

MEZOKE, WE HAVE TO REMAIN VIGILANT WITH THE RAPAKHUN...

WE NEED TO KNOW FOR CERTAIN IF THESE NOMADS ARE HIDING SOMETHING FROM US.

HECTOR, MAKE SURE THAT THE MALAYSIAN MILITARY WILL STAY WITH US...

THEY NEED TO KEEP THE MEN THEY ARRESTED ISOLATED.

IT'S ESSENTIAL THAT THEY HAVE NO CONTACT WITH THE PRESS. ONLY OUR VERSION OF EVENTS MUST BE HEARD.

AND THEN, WE'RE GOING TO NEED REINFORCEMENTS...

A TEAM WE CAN TRUST...

... TO GO TO DEHADATO.

THE LAST PLANET THESE NOMADS VISITED.

BESIDES...

I'M SURE THEY'LL LOVE THAT.